Contents

Welcome

Durham Cathedral is the [...] England, perhaps even in [...] its architecture but also for [...] incomparable setting. For this reason it was inscribed together with the Castle as one of Britain's first World Heritage Sites. In a nationwide BBC poll held in 2001 it was voted the nation's best-loved building. Like Hadrian's Wall and the Angel of the North, it is an icon of north-east England, its image instantly recognisable to people who love this part of Britain.

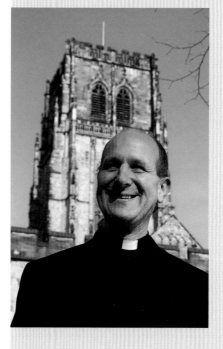

As an enduring monument to human skill and inventiveness, the Cathedral speaks powerfully of heritage and history. Its sheer size and splendour testify to the power of Norman overlords establishing their authority in the land they had conquered. Yet it was primarily built as a religious building: as the shrine of a humble saint, as a destination for pilgrims and as home for a community of worship, learning and practical care. It was built for the glory of God.

In a new millennium, with its anxieties about the future of humanity and its uncertain attitude to religion, the Cathedral continues to stand both as a sign of our human search and of divine welcome and hospitality. It points to the reality of God in the life of this world and to the new possibilities held out to us in the gospel. I hope your visit here brings you joy.

Michael Sadgrove

*The Very Reverend Michael Sadgrove,
Dean of Durham*

Introduction

Durham Cathedral has been described as 'one of the great architectural experiences of Europe'. To approach the city by train is to enjoy one of the most remarkable views in Britain. From the station, we take in at a glance what it is that makes Durham unique: the Cathedral and Castle positioned on an acropolis surrounded by the River Wear with the medieval city gathered at its feet. All the historic functions of this site are clear: defensive military fortification, religious shrine, academy and market place.

The Cathedral is renowned as a masterpiece of Romanesque (or Norman) architecture, the style brought from France to Britain through the Norman conquest of 1066. It was begun in 1093 and largely completed within 40 years. Durham is one of a handful of English cathedrals to have preserved the unity and integrity of its original design, and the only one that retains almost all of its Norman craftsmanship.

Why was the Cathedral built? What was it *for*?

A first answer is, for the glory of God, for the Cathedral is above all else a place of worship. But it was specifically constructed to house the shrine of the North's best-loved saint, Cuthbert, in honour of whom pilgrims came to Durham from all over England. His story is inextricably intertwined with the

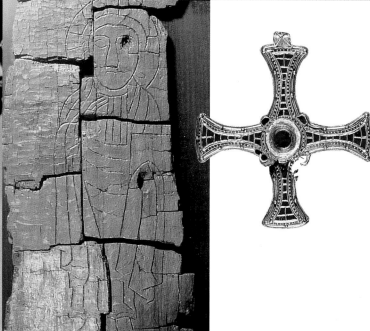

entire history of the Cathedral. It was also the home of a
Benedictine monastic community. But it served a political and
military function too by reinforcing the authority of the prince-
bishops over England's northern border. Hence Sir Walter
Scott's much quoted epithet, 'half church of God, half castle
'gainst the Scot'.

Today, the Cathedral continues to be a place of prayer and
pilgrimage, an icon of the North-East, the seat of the Bishop of
Durham and a focal point for the life of the Church in the region.

A tour of the building

As we walk round Durham Cathedral, we are following in the steps of millions of pilgrims. It is important to understand that one of the principal purposes for which the church was built was as a sacred space in which people would walk, either in solemn procession during acts of worship, or as crowds of pilgrims, or as individuals making their way towards the shrine of St Cuthbert.

Our visit takes us into the Cathedral from Palace Green. We move eastward up the nave to the crossing beneath the tower, and beyond it, into the quire. We reach the emotional and spiritual climax of the building with the shrine behind the high altar where Cuthbert lies buried. Returning to the west end we enter the Galilee Chapel where we find another shrine, that of the Venerable Bede. From there we leave the church to enter the cloister, around which are grouped the buildings of the Benedictine monastery, a remarkable survival from the Middle Ages.

Our tour will describe the architectural features of the building and its main monuments and furnishings. But it will also interpret its meaning both for past generations and as a working Cathedral today.

ABOVE Detail of the carved stonework above the north door showing the characteristic Norman zig-zag pattern
BELOW LEFT The main entrance to the Cathedral through the north door

Entering the Cathedral

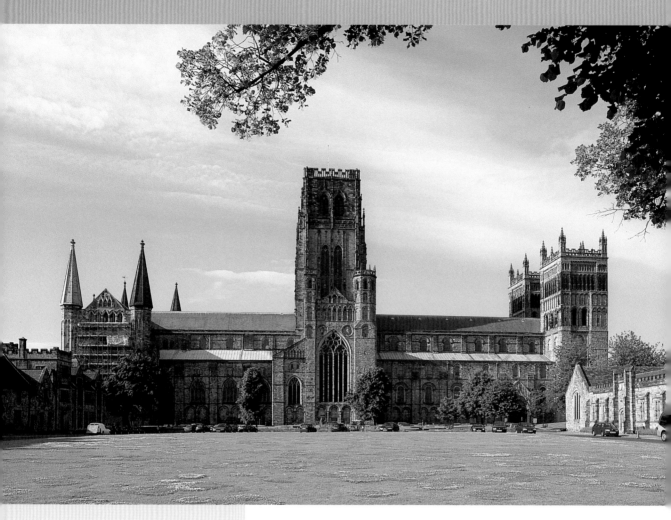

ABOVE The Cathedral from Palace Green

BELOW Replica of the sanctuary knocker. The original is in the Treasures of St Cuthbert exhibition

The 'show' front of the Cathedral is the Palace Green side. The huge mass of the building (total length 496 feet/143 metres) closes in the entire south side of the Green, balancing if not overshadowing the Castle opposite. The exterior marks out the different components of the Cathedral: a Norman **nave** and **quire** with **transepts** between; beyond the quire a 13th-century Gothic extension, the **Chapel of the Nine Altars**; and beyond the western towers a late Norman extension, the 12th-century **Galilee Chapel**.

The western towers, built above the precipitous gorge of the river, date from the 12th and 13th centuries. The great central tower (218 feet/66 metres in height) was the last major addition to the fabric, displaying fine late 15th-century perpendicular Gothic detail.

The sanctuary knocker on the main door is a replica of the famous 12th-century original which is now in the Treasures of St Cuthbert exhibition. Until 1623 when the right of sanctuary was abolished, those being pursued for certain crimes could enter the Cathedral by grasping hold of the ring and be offered a safe place or 'sanctuary' for 37 days. After that they would be required to leave the country or face trial.

The Nave

On entering the Cathedral, we need to take in the whole before examining the parts. This is best done by sitting down near the entrance with the length of the church stretching ahead of us.

The church was designed as a building with a succession of rooms or spaces, each with its distinct function. The **nave** (Latin *navis*, 'ship') is the body of the church where ordinary people were free to enter and where large Cathedral services take place to this day. We must imagine it without seating, for this was a space for crowds to attend services or walk in procession. At the head of the nave is the **crossing** under the central tower. Here there would once have been

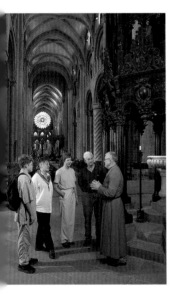

a screen separating the people's nave from the **quire** reserved for the daily worship of the monastic community. At the far end we glimpse the **sanctuary** and within it the **high altar**. Behind this, not visible from the nave, is the shrine of St Cuthbert.

The nave is much as it was nine centuries ago. The great **piers**, marching eastwards on either side, convey an impression of immensity, antiquity and trustworthiness. Moreover, they reinforce the sense that the Cathedral is a sequence of thresholds that leads the eye and the pilgrim from one room to the next, a journey that culminates in the high altar and the rose window above. The **compound piers** mark the division of the nave into rectangular bays, as we can see if we follow the columns upwards to the stone vault. The round **drum piers** with their carved geometric patterns are a sculptural

'triforium' The middle storey of a church housing a wall-passage above the aisle and below the *clerestory*

FAR LEFT
The Cathedral's
Ministry of
Welcome
LEFT The nave,
looking east
RIGHT One of the
great pillars, also
known as 'piers'
BELOW RIGHT
A lunchtime concert
by a local school
BOTTOM The rose
window at the
eastern end of the
Cathedral

OVERLEAF
The nave
and vaulting,
looking east

tour de force, possibly a Durham innovation. Their eye-catching designs of chevrons, vertical fluting and lozenges are matched in pairs across the nave. This counterpoint between large-scale effect and small-scale attention to detail is carried through the entire building, for instance, in the chevron decoration that adorns many of the arches and vault ribs, the capitals to the piers and the intersecting patterns of the **blind arcading** on the walls of the aisles.

The proportions of the nave are carefully contrived to balance the two effects the builders wished to create. On the one hand, they wanted to emphasise the great length of the church. They adopted the standard three-storey elevation common in Norman churches: the nave **arcade** itself (the series of round-headed arches on each side), the **triforium** above, and at the top level the **clerestory**. Highlighted by the lines of the string courses above and beneath the gallery, these strongly emphasise the horizontal aspect of the building. Counterbalancing this is the equally powerful vertical thrust provided by the piers, especially the compound piers that run directly from floor to vault and intersect with the horizontals. The mathematics of these proportions is no accident, and explains why the nave is so satisfying a space. It is light enough to lift the eye and the spirit. It is substantial enough to connect the parts to the whole and anchor it to the earth on which it stands.

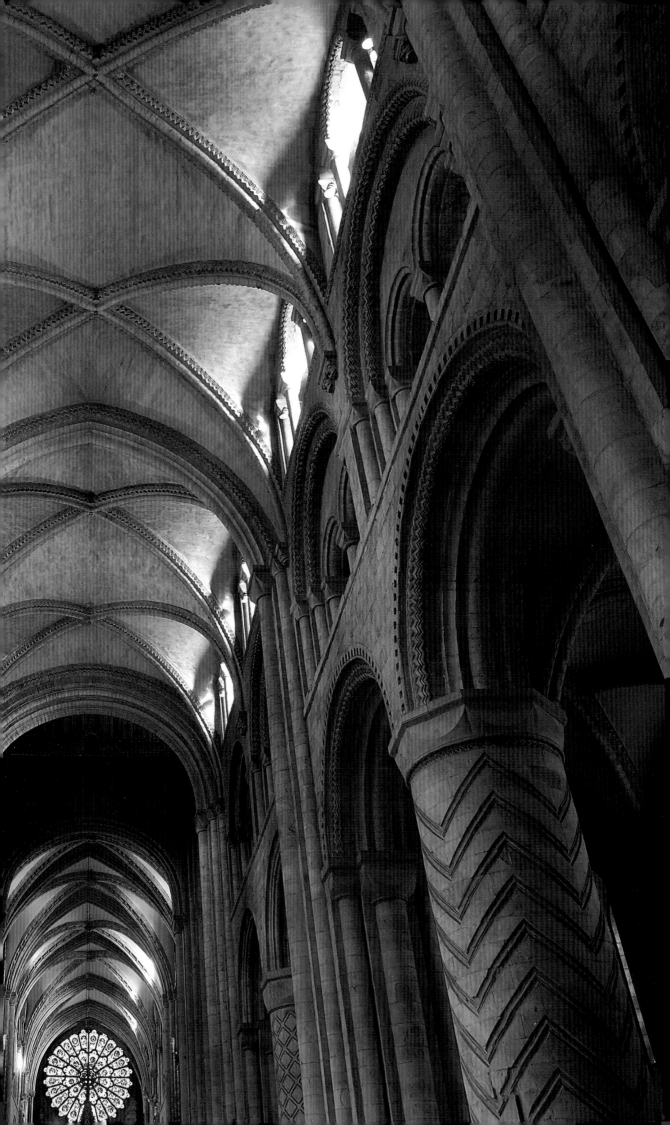

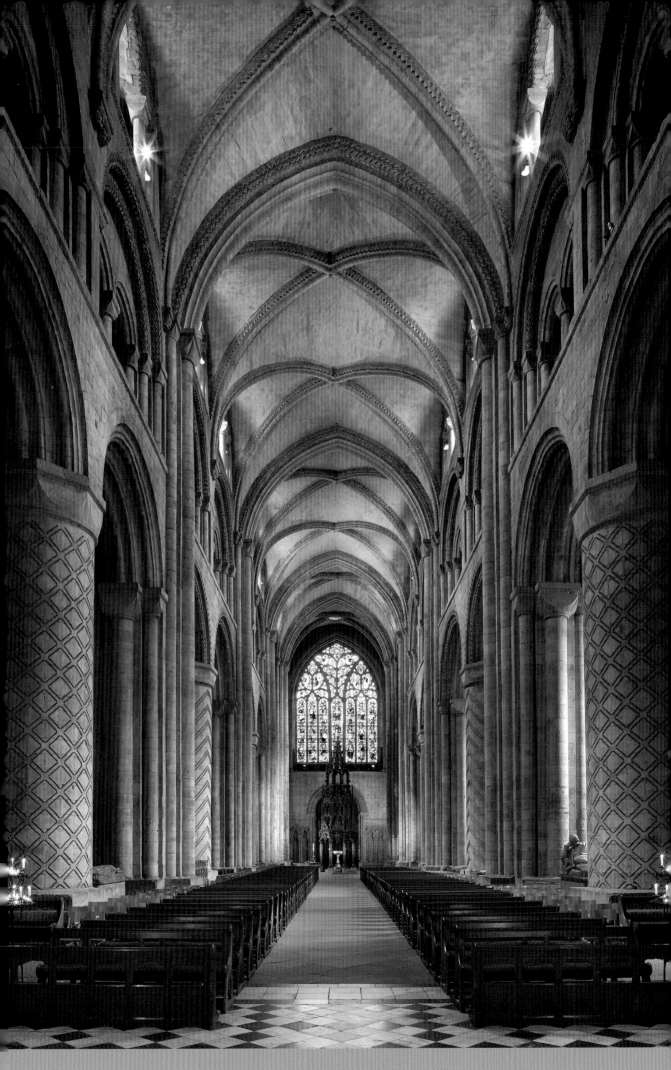

The nave reveals the ground-breaking character of this extraordinary building. It was here at Durham that for the first time in England masons solved the engineering problem of how to throw a stone vault safely across such a large space. The nave **vault** is entirely Norman work, completed in 1133. But the arches that spring from the great compound piers on either side to span the width of the nave are pointed, not round-headed like those of the arcades, the gallery and the clerestory which we associate with Norman architecture. The pointed arch is a much more efficient load-bearing structure than the round-headed arch. Together, the pointed arches and the diagonal ribs that criss-cross the vault enabled the nave to be constructed entirely of stone. To span a width of 32 feet/10 metres with a vault rising to 75 feet/23 metres was a pioneering achievement that paved the way for the emergence of the Gothic style in the next century.

The most important piece of furniture in the nave is the **font**, close to the main entrance. This is the place of Christian initiation, where children and adults are admitted into membership of the Church through baptism. Traditionally, the font is placed near the door of the church as a symbol of entrance and belonging. Standing at the west end of the building,

ABOVE The font
LEFT The nave, looking west
FAR RIGHT Preparing the font for a baptism
RIGHT Detail of the top of the font cover

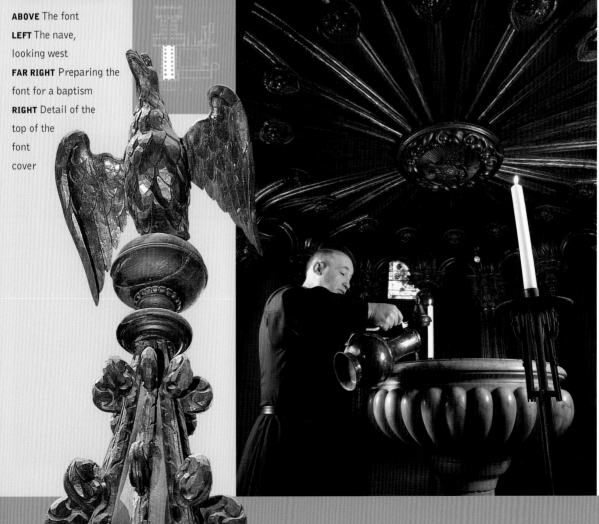

11

The Nave

it mirrors the other principal focal point of the church, the **high altar** at the east end. So the entire length of the church is poised between the font as the place of beginnings and the altar as the place of climax and consummation. The nave is a symbol of the journey of religious faith and human experience.

Specifically, the font stands for the central affirmations of Christian faith summed up in the creed that is recited at every baptism. Round the font is a large gathering space which allows a congregation to witness the baptism liturgy, but is also a sign that the nave is a place where the baptised people of God gather together for worship. The marble bowl for the water of baptism dates from 1663. The magnificent **font cover** is of the same period, a fine example of the luscious woodwork throughout the building dating from the time of the 17th-century Bishop of Durham, John Cosin. It is 40 feet/12 metres high, one of the tallest in the land.

The **organ case** near the south door dates from a little later in the 17th century and originally stood over the quire screen. The **miners' memorial** east of the door also includes woodwork from this screen. It was created in 1947 as a symbol of Durham Cathedral's long association with the mining industry and as a reminder of its human cost.

ABOVE Natural patterns in sandstone piers
LEFT The west (Fossor) window depicting the family tree of King David
BELOW The miners' memorial and working safety lamp

REMEMBER BEFORE GOD THE DURHAM MINERS WHO HAVE GIVEN THEIR LIVES IN THE PITS OF THIS COUNTY AND THOSE WHO WORK IN DARKNESS AND DANGER IN THOSE PITS TODAY

Burials were discouraged in a building overshadowed by the presence of Cuthbert's burial place, so there are few monuments in the nave. This creates an impression of uncluttered simplicity and restraint within architecture of such nobility. In the south arcade is the impressive **tomb-chest** of 1388 belonging to John, Lord Neville, a wealthy benefactor of the Cathedral Priory.

Nearby is the mutilated monument of his father Ralph, the first layman to be given the honour of a Cathedral burial for his victorious part in the Battle of Neville's Cross in 1346. Opposite is a memorial dated 1839 to a local headmaster, James Britton, whose relaxed posture makes an interesting foil to the formality of the architecture.

Among the **windows**, Prior Fossor's great 14th-century west window shows how well the mature Gothic style harmonises with the Romanesque. Its coloured glass, as with many of the windows, is Victorian. At the west end of the aisles are 20th-century windows depicting Cuthbert and King Oswald of Northumbria, whose head is buried with Cuthbert's remains. The colourful 'Daily Bread' window near the north door was given by the Durham branch of Marks and Spencer in 1984 to mark the centenary of the business. It is an abstract interpretation of the Last Supper at which Jesus broke bread with his disciples before his death.

ABOVE Blind arcading showing reproduction medieval painted decoration
ABOVE RIGHT The 19th-century great west doors
RIGHT Part of the 17th-century organ case

Medieval churches were usually built on a west-east axis, so that worshippers faced not only the high altar but also the rising sun and the holy city of Jerusalem, symbols of the resurrection of Christ and of the heavenly city promised to the faithful. Like many churches, the original Norman Cathedral had a 'footprint' shaped like a Latin cross, though this was later added to. The arms of the cross are known as **transepts**, extensions to the building on the north and south sides.

The south transept contains one of the Cathedral's most famous curiosities, the highly coloured **medieval clock**. It was originally constructed by Prior Castell in the late 15th or early 16th century but altered in the 17th. It was taken down in 1845 as it was thought by the Victorians to be too frivolous for a serious building like a cathedral. Its reconstruction as a working clock in 1938 was the first of many projects by the recently founded Friends of the Cathedral.

The **chapel** in the transept was furnished in 1924 as a memorial to the Durham Light Infantry, whose standards are arrayed above, and whose battle honours are recorded here alongside books of remembrance. On the west wall opposite hangs a **miners' banner**, another link with the working traditions of the North-East. Below the banner is a memorial to Bishop Shute Barrington who died in 1826, a fine piece of sculpture in white marble by the renowned Sheffield sculptor Francis Chantrey.

TOP LEFT Bishop Barrington's memorial
LEFT The Moses window
ABOVE Prior Castell's clock

RIGHT The Durham
Light Infantry
Chapel
BELOW RIGHT The
'Te Deum' window
in the south transept
**BELOW AND BOTTOM
RIGHT**
Regimental books
of remembrance
for the Durham
Light Infantry
BOTTOM Regimental
colours

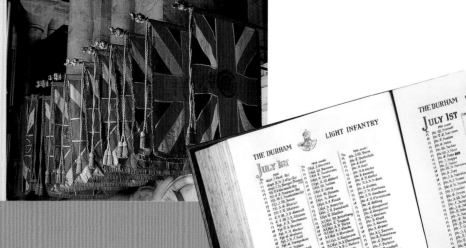

The Tower and Crossing

At the **crossing** we can appreciate the spatial qualities of the Cathedral. Here the east-west and north-south axes of the church meet, a point of rest around which the principal spaces of the Norman church are organised. The view westwards down the nave is especially beautiful, particularly when the setting sun lights up the great west window. The transepts north and south balance the length of the church, while eastwards the crossing marks a clear threshold as the gateway to the quire. And to look upwards is to appreciate for the first time the height of the **lantern**, the interior of the 15th-century tower. The crown of the tower vault is 155 ft/47 metres high. Above this are the ringing chamber and **belfry**. Visitors may climb the 325 steps to the top of the tower: access is from the south transept. The view of Durham, the wooded loop of the Wear and the surrounding countryside is well worth the effort.

The furnishings in the crossing form a Gothic-revival group by the Victorian architect George Gilbert Scott. His three-arched **screen** stands on the site of the medieval **pulpitum** that

ABOVE Visitors by the Scott lectern
TOP LEFT Detail from the quire screen
LEFT The Miners' Festival service viewed from the lantern

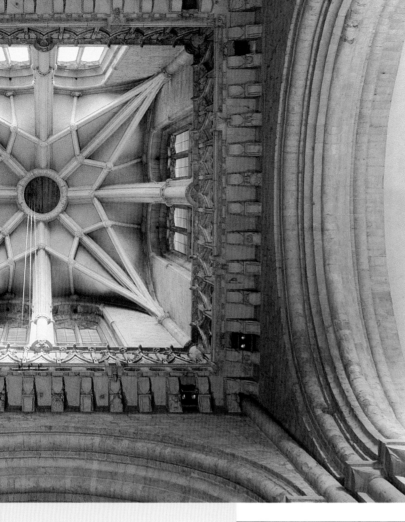

enclosed the monastic quire. Its successor, Cosin's 17th-century organ screen, was removed in the early 19th century to open up an uninterrupted vista towards the high altar. Far from serving to ennoble the interior, this unfortunate action merely created the effect of a long tunnel. To remedy this, the

ABOVE Looking upwards in the central tower

TOP RIGHT The tower staircase

RIGHT The Gilbert Scott pulpit, screen and lectern

BELOW Cathedral vergers undertaking routine cleaning

screen was installed in 1876. This, and the **nave pulpit** of the same time, were greatly admired in their day but how well their sumptuous marble fits in this sandstone building has generated much debate since. Scott's brass **lectern**, a copy of the lectern that once stood here in the Middle Ages, depicts a pelican in her piety. She is shown piercing her breast to feed her young with her blood, an ancient symbol of the Christ who through his death nourishes his people. The lectern and pulpit are the visible focus of the proclamation of the word of God in worship.

'pulpitum' The stone screen that divided the *quire* of a great church from the nave

'quire (or choir)' The space east of the nave where the daily monastic services were sung

The **quire**, and beyond it the **sanctuary**, were the heart of the medieval church. Here, in a space once entirely enclosed by the pulpitum, stalls and screens, the monks of the Cathedral Priory

would gather seven times each day to sing the divine office. This offering of daily praise and prayer was known as the *opus Dei*, the work of God. Around it the whole of monastic life was organised. In 1539 the monastery was dissolved by order of Henry VIII, one of the last foundations to be suppressed in England, and in 1541 the Cathedral was refounded as an Anglican institution. The cycle of daily worship continued in the Reformed style familiar to us now as the services of morning and evening prayer in the *Book of Common Prayer* of the Church of England. Apart from the Civil War (1649-1660) when the Cathedral was closed for worship, this rhythm has continued each day ever since, with the choir of boys and men now singing evensong six days each week during term-time together with Sunday morning matins and sung eucharist, the principal service of the week.

As was usual in a medieval church building, the Cathedral was constructed from east to west so that the high altar and the shrine of St Cuthbert could be installed as soon as possible and worship and pilgrimage could begin. The east end of the church down to the crossing was complete by 1104, although the quire

ABOVE Intricate carving above the stalls
LEFT Quire pulpit hanging designed by Leonard Childs
BELOW The highly decorated organ pipes
RIGHT The quire, looking east. The floor is by George Gilbert Scott

'sanctuary' The space east of the quire that houses the high altar where the sacrament of the Eucharist (the Mass or Holy Communion) is celebrated

vault we now see dates only from the 13th century, following the failure of the original Norman vault.

But the appearance of the quire at ground level now feels to be more of the 17th than the 12th century, dominated as it is by the elaborate carved woodwork of Bishop Cosin's **stalls**. These were made in 1665, not long after the Cathedral had been restored as a place of worship at the end of the Civil War. Their tall 'Gothic' canopies seem to have been inspired by the medieval stone screen behind the altar, but interpreted in a way that belongs entirely to the Renaissance. The skilled craftsmen who worked on them also created furnishings for several parish churches in County Durham. The Latin inscriptions are inspired by the Old Testament; their theme is the praise of God through music. The seats of the canons' stalls (as they originally were) in the back row have beautifully carved **misericords** beneath. The quire pulpit carries a hanging designed by Leonard Childs and executed by the Cathedral Broderers. It depicts the traditional symbols of the four evangelists: the man of St Matthew, the lion of St Mark, the ox of St Luke and the eagle of St John.

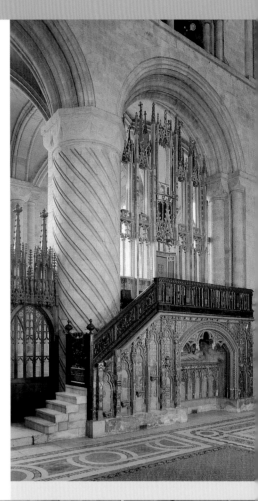

The **organ** was originally built by 'Father' Willis in 1876, replacing the famous Father Smith organ of 1686 that had stood over the quire screen. (Some of the organ case survives near the west end.) In 1905 the Willis instrument was rebuilt by the Durham firm of organ builders Harrison and Harrison, who continue to care for it today. A four-manual instrument, it is one of the finest Romantic organs of England.

FAR LEFT Detail from the gate leading to the Bishop's throne
LEFT The Bishop's throne (cathedra)
BELOW LEFT The ornate tomb of Bishop Hatfield beneath the cathedra

ABOVE, BELOW LEFT AND RIGHT The choir rehearsing for one of the 344 regular services at which it sings each year

Beyond the stalls on the south side stands the **Bishop's throne**. A cathedral is so called because it houses the Bishop's seat or *cathedra* that symbolises his ministry of teaching, pastoral care and evangelism in his diocese. This extraordinary, highly decorated piece was designed by Bishop Hatfield (died 1381) as both his throne and his tomb. His episcopate was perhaps the high water mark of the Durham Palatinate, whose prince-bishops exercised not only spiritual but also political jurisdiction, with powers to mint coinage, raise an army and hear cases at law. Only in the early 19th century were these 'temporal' powers of the prince-bishops finally absorbed into the Crown.

21

The Sanctuary

East of the quire lies the **sanctuary**. It houses the **high altar**, the principal focus of the church. Here the sacrament of the Eucharist (the Mass or Holy Communion) is celebrated, the bread and wine representing Christ's body and blood given for the world. It is the place of recognition and gift for the people of God, where the journey begun at the font reaches its culmination.

The sanctuary is marked out as this point of climax by the great stone **reredos** behind the altar. This, the Neville Screen, is one of the treasures of Durham Cathedral. It was largely the gift of John, Lord Neville whose tomb-chest is in the nave. Completed in 1380 out of

stone thought to have come from Caen in northern France, it would originally have been brightly painted, and statues of angels and saints would have stood in each of the 107 niches. All this was swept away in the years that followed the Reformation. (The alabaster figures, it is said, were buried by the monks before they could be destroyed; if so, their whereabouts remain one of the great mysteries of Durham.) The screen is still impressive today for the purity of its stone and the simplicity of its Gothic lines. On either side of the altar, incorporated into the screen, are the **sedilia**, stone seats for those assisting at services at the high altar.

The high altar itself is modern, but within it stands a modest 17th-century marble altar that is used during Holy Week, the annual celebration of the death of Jesus. The coloured patterned marble **pavement** in the quire and sanctuary is again the work of Scott, of a piece with his pulpit and screen at the crossing.

FAR LEFT View through the Neville Screen
LEFT Detail of the Neville Screen
ABOVE Stonework near the high altar
BELOW Carving symbolising good devouring evil
RIGHT The high altar, and behind it, the Neville Screen

The South Quire Aisle

The Shrine of St Cuthbert

LEFT The south quire aisle, looking east, showing the rear of Bishop Hatfield's tomb with the cathedra above

Behind the high altar, reached by steps from the quire aisles, lies the **Shrine of St Cuthbert**. He is buried beneath a simple stone slab that bears his name in Latin: CVTHBERTVS. Nearby is a mutilated 15th-century statue of Cuthbert holding the head of the Northumbrian King Oswald. Above is a 20th-century canopy by Ninian Comper depicting Christ in glory. On either side are contemporary banners by Thetis Blacker of Cuthbert and Oswald. Candles and kneelers invite contemplation at the shrine of one of England's most remarkable men.

Cuthbert, a Northumbrian, was born in about 634. A guardian of sheep in the Scottish border hill country, he entered the monastery at Melrose, later moving to the 'holy island' of Lindisfarne, first as prior to the community there, then in 685 as bishop. It was here that the Irish monk Aidan (died 651) had established a monastery as the headquarters of his mission to reconvert Northumbria to Christianity at the invitation of King Oswald (*c.* 605–642).

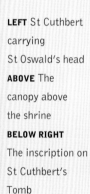

LEFT St Cuthbert carrying St Oswald's head
ABOVE The canopy above the shrine
BELOW RIGHT The inscription on St Cuthbert's Tomb

Cuthbert's holiness, learning and love of nature, his care for people and the fervour of his preaching were already legendary in his lifetime. He had established a hermitage on the island of Inner Farne where he died in 687. He was buried on Lindisfarne. Eleven years later his body was disinterred and found to be undecayed, whereupon his shrine was set up on Lindisfarne. This was Northumbria's golden age, and its cultural and intellectual achievement is demonstrated in the Lindisfarne Gospels, written there early in the 8th century 'in honour of God and St Cuthbert'.

By the 9th century, Viking raids drove the 'community of St Cuthbert' to seek a new, more secure, home. The community, carrying the relics of Cuthbert and the Lindisfarne Gospels, started a long journey round the north of England. They came to Chester-le-Street in 883 where they rested for over a century. In 995, having stayed briefly at Ripon, they arrived in Durham. Legend says that as they approached the peninsula, the cart bearing the coffin stuck fast in the ground. Some women were

The Shrine of St Cuthbert

overheard talking about a lost cow. 'Dun Holm' was mentioned as the place where the animal would be found. This was taken as a sign from Cuthbert, so the coffin was duly brought on to the peninsula where it has remained ever since.

The community's first church on the site lasted less than 100 years. In 1083 a Benedictine convent was founded in place of the Saxon community, and a decade later the Norman Cathedral was begun as a more splendid house for the shrine. Cuthbert's relics were installed in their present position in 1104. Durham rapidly became the foremost pilgrimage destination in England, and one of the wealthiest. Only with the martyrdom of Thomas Becket in 1170 did Canterbury eclipse it, although Durham's energetic promotion of the pilgrimage ensured that the shrine continued to attract pilgrims throughout the Middle Ages.

LEFT Detail of St Cuthbert's pectoral cross
ABOVE Rare gold thread and silk Saxon embroidery found in St Cuthbert's coffin
RIGHT The Shrine of St Cuthbert

In late 1537, the King's commissioners came to Durham to dismantle the shrine. It was stripped of its gold, silver and jewels and levelled to the ground. When Cuthbert's coffin was uncovered, they found not dust and bones but a body in priestly vestments 'fresh, safe and not consumed'. As a result it was left alone and re-interred. The grave has twice been opened up since then, in 1827 and 1899. The precious artefacts from Cuthbert's time removed in 1827 are now on display in the Treasures of St Cuthbert exhibition. The stark black slab that bears his name is, perhaps, as eloquent a tribute to the simple prior, bishop and hermit of Lindisfarne as his elaborately jewelled shrine had once been.

In 2005, St Cuthbert's name was reinstated in the legal dedication of the cathedral from which it had been removed in the 16th century. It is now dedicated to 'Christ, Blessed Mary the Virgin and St Cuthbert'.

LEFT The remains of St Cuthbert's coffin
ABOVE Lindisfarne Priory

The Chapel of the Nine Altars

At the east end the Cathedral opens up unexpectedly around us. A line on the floor of the **feretory** indicates the curved apse with which the east end of the Cathedral originally ended. As numbers of pilgrims grew, it became necessary to enlarge the space around Cuthbert's shrine to accommodate them. This was done between 1242 and 1280.

The Chapel of the Nine Altars is as pure a piece of Early English Gothic architecture as the nave is Norman. The 'join' happens in the easternmost bay of the quire, though the entire quire vault also dates from this period. The resemblance to the Early English cathedral at Salisbury is no accident: it was Bishop le Poore of Salisbury who instigated the work on his translation to Durham. The chapel spreading into eastern transepts was modelled on Fountains Abbey in Yorkshire. The vertical thrust of this place is emphasised by a lower floor level, the tall lancet windows and the slender shafts of Frosterley marble running from floor to vault. This vault gave the masons some trouble, for on the south side the ribs 'miss' a central roof boss.

The **rose window** is a late 18th-century reworking of a medieval predecessor. The beautiful **Joseph window** on the north end has double tracery straddling the wall passage in between. The 'nine' altars originally stood against the east wall, enabling the priest members of the convent to celebrate mass at an altar each day. The central altar of St Aidan has hangings made by the Broderers depicting the northern saints. The altars to Hild (left) and Margaret of Scotland (right) commemorate women saints associated with the North-East. The hangings on the Margaret altar were completed by the Cathedral Broderers in 2005. The painting near the St Margaret altar is by Paula Rego. It was commissioned by the Cathedral and dedicated in 2004. It shows the saint near the end of her life, together with her son David, future king of Scotland, himself one of the Scotland's best loved saints. A marble statue commemorates Bishop Van Mildert, the last of the prince-bishops who with the Cathedral Chapter founded the University of Durham in 1832. Other bishops and deans are commemorated on ledger stones in the floor.

ABOVE Memorial to Bishop Van Mildert
LEFT 'Frosterley Marble' showing characteristic fossils
BELOW LEFT AND BELOW St Margaret altar frontal, and painting by Paula Rego
RIGHT The Chapel of the Nine Altars

'feretory' A shrine in which the relics of a saint are housed

The **quire aisles** lead from the Chapel of the Nine Altars to the transepts. In the wall of the north aisle are the **bedesmen's benches** (from the Old English *bede*, meaning a prayer). These lay people have for centuries played a key role in the daily life of the Cathedral, not least in its worship. Opposite is a monument to a great Victorian Bishop, Joseph Lightfoot (died 1889), one of the most learned theologians of his day.

Like the south transept, the north transept has a chapel behind the Norman piers. The **Gregory Chapel** (formerly the Benedict Chapel – two of the three medieval chapels in this area were dedicated to these saints) was refurbished in the 20th century for personal prayer, and the sacrament is reserved there. The **altar**, on a moveable plinth against the north wall of the transept, is used in the crossing at major Cathedral services. It is dedicated to St Benedict, whose rule for monks was followed in the Middle Ages in thousands of Benedictine houses across Europe such as Durham, and continues to be observed in monasteries to this day. A **banner** on the wall marks the link between the Dioceses of Durham and Lesotho in southern Africa. The curious white marble monument just inside the quire aisle is of Matthew Woodifield (died 1826).

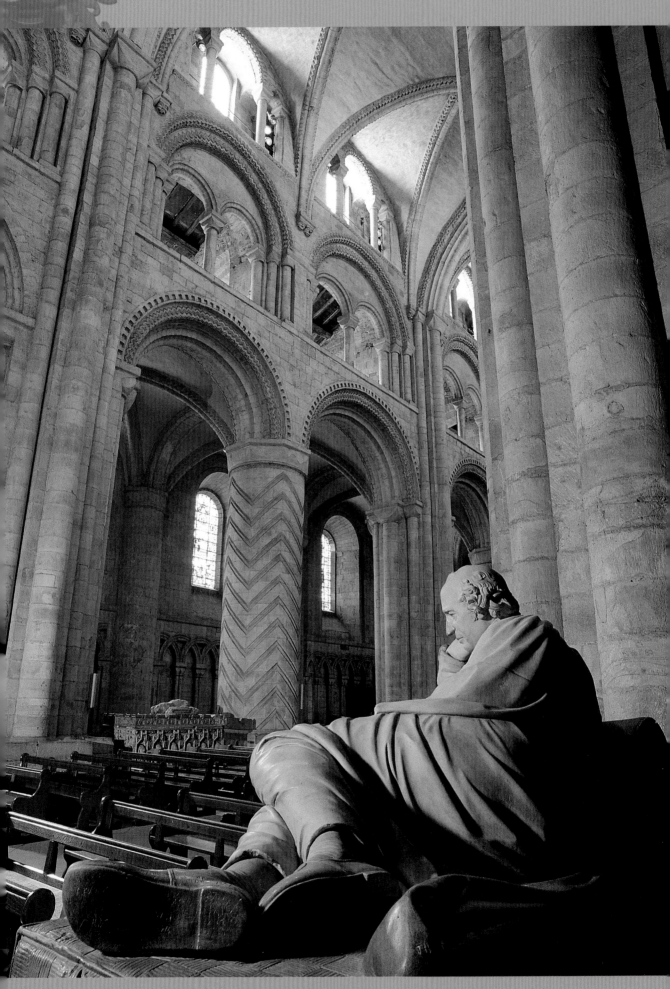

The Galilee Chapel and the Venerable Bede

As we walk west down the nave, we cross a **line in black marble** on the floor near the font. This marked a boundary which women were forbidden to cross, for this church belonged to an all-male Benedictine community. An early attempt to build a Lady Chapel for women east of the shrine was aborted owing to the instability of the foundations. In 1170, Bishop Hugh le Puiset (sometimes known as Pudsey) began to construct a Lady Chapel at the opposite end of the Cathedral. This is the **Galilee Chapel**, entered through doors in the west wall, and one of the most exquisite parts of the building.

The Galilee is partly a chapel, partly a porch or narthex, a place to assemble before and after services. Such porches are common in Romanesque churches in France, such as Vézelay. Galilee was the homeland of Jesus, from where he 'went up' to Jerusalem, so the Galilee Chapel was a place of arrival from which to enter the main Cathedral. But Galilee is also where the risen Jesus promises to go ahead of the disciples to meet them. So the Galilee Chapel was also a place of departure and dismissal, and great Cathedral services and processions would often have ended here.

LEFT The nave with the tomb of James Britton, a 19th-century headmaster of Durham School
ABOVE Communion is regularly celebrated in the Galilee Chapel
RIGHT The Last Supper table by Colin Wilbourn
ABOVE RIGHT Wall painting believed to depict St Cuthbert

The Galilee is still Norman, with its four arcades of round arches decorated with elaborate chevrons. But it is much lighter in feel than the nave, and its air of luminous transparency suggests that the Gothic era is not far away. Some see in the architecture of this chapel an echo of the great mosque at Córdoba in Spain. Here the original **great west doorway** into the Cathedral can be seen, blocked since the 15th century by the altar and **tomb-chest** of Thomas Langley, Cardinal and twice Chancellor of England (died 1437). The **painting** of the crucifixion has been attributed to the 16th-century Flemish painter Van Orley. On the north side of the Galilee are important **wall paintings**. On the wall behind the modern altar are a bishop and a king, almost certainly St Cuthbert and St Oswald. These date from around the time of the Galilee's construction in the 12th century. Above the arcade is a later series of paintings from the 13th or 14th centuries: the crucifixion of Christ, and the apostles as martyrs shown dying for their faith. Fragments of 14th- and 15th-century stained glass from all over the Cathedral are preserved in the windows.

ABOVE Bede window
RIGHT Annunciation by Joseph Pyrz
BELOW The wall painting above the arcade

The Galilee Chapel and the Venerable Bede

Like the feretory, the Galilee holds a firm place in the affection of people across the North-East for the shrine it contains. A simple Latin inscription on a **tomb-chest** identifies its contents as the bones of the Venerable Bede. It is thanks to Bede's writings that we know so much about the Church in England in Saxon times, and in particular about St Cuthbert. Known as the 'father of English history', Bede was born in about 673. As a boy of seven he joined the Saxon community at Wearmouth, being transferred to the newly founded monastery of Jarrow soon afterwards. Here he spent the rest of his life. He was the most accomplished scholar of his day as historian, theologian, poet, scientist, biographer and supremely as author of many commentaries on the Bible. Like the Lindisfarne Gospels, his writings show the heights achieved by the flowering of Northumbrian civilisation in the 8th century.

Bede died in 735 at Jarrow, where he was buried. In about 1022 his relics were stolen (or removed for safe keeping) by a Durham monk and brought to the Cathedral, where they were placed with Cuthbert's. Later on, after the construction of the Galilee Chapel, they were placed there in a shrine of their own. It too survived the Dissolution and, as in the case of Cuthbert, the simplicity of his tomb as we now see it is an apt comment on the humility of Bede's life. The recess behind has a quotation from Bede's commentary on the Apocalypse (or Book of Revelation), praising 'Christ the morning star'. It was designed by Frank Roper and George Pace in 1971. This inscription is interpreted in the lamp above the tomb, designed by Christopher Downes, and given by Rotarians in 2005.

The wooden **statue** of Mary by the 20th-century Polish sculptor Joseph Pyrz marks the Galilee as the Lady Chapel. The square Last Supper table has a marquetry top that unfolds to reveal wooden sculptures of emblems of the Eucharist. It was made by the contemporary sculptor Colin Wilbourn.

LEFT A page from Bede's **Life of Cuthbert**
BELOW Part of the inscription on Bede's tomb
BOTTOM St Paul's, Jarrow
RIGHT Bede's tomb

The Norman doorways of Durham
are a study in themselves. The south-
west door is worth stopping to
admire from the outside, both for its
medieval timber and ironwork, and
for the Romanesque decoration of
its portal. On turning left into the
cloister we come to another fine
example, the **Prior's Door**.

The cloister was the hub of the
monastery's daily life and linked its
principal working buildings. Durham
is fortunate that so much survived
the Dissolution, for even today this
part of the Cathedral conveys a sense
of how the activities of the monastery
were inseparably connected to one
another and to the community's
principal purpose, the daily worship
of God. Originally the cloister was
glassed in. Here the monks washed
(the stone basin in the middle of the
grass is what remains of their
lavabo), exercised, taught, studied,

and copied manuscripts, music and liturgical books. The cloister was laid out when the Cathedral was begun, though much of it now dates from the 15th century and later.

Clockwise from the Prior's Door, the next entrance leads into the **slype***, once a simple passage, later the monks' parlour. The room above is the choir's practice room or song school. Next door is the **Chapter House***, a large and important room where the daily business of the monastery was transacted, the monks sitting on stone benches set into the walls. It is so called because each day, a 'chapter' of the monastic rule was read aloud to the community. Here too their successors in the re-founded Cathedral, the Dean and Chapter, conducted their affairs. The first Norman bishops of Durham are buried underneath the floor and commemorated in 20th-century stained glass. This was said to be the finest Norman chapter house in England before its partial demolition in 1796 to create a warmer environment for 18th-century clergy. It was rebuilt in the original style in 1895. Off the Chapter House, the **sacristy***, uniquely for such a room, turns out to have been the monastic **prison**.

The last door but one on this side of the cloister gives on to the original monastic **night stair*** used by monks to go from their dormitory to the church for night services. The first monks' dormitory was sited here while construction of the Cathedral began. When the dormitory was later moved nearer the church, the Priors, appointed to lead the convent, established themselves on the site. The **Prior's Lodging***,

LEFT AND BELOW
Anglo Saxon stones displayed in the monks' dormitory
ABOVE The roof of the monks' dormitory

now the Deanery, contains some of the oldest fabric on the peninsula. Some idea of the sturdy solidity of this 11th-century work can be glimpsed in the vaulted **undercrofts** now used for audio-visual and exhibition purposes.

The Benedictine rule emphasised the importance of study, and monasteries were the focus of much of the intellectual life of the Middle Ages. The library now occupies the former monastic refectory and dormitory over the south and west walks.

The **refectory*** has an elegant 17th-century interior and contains part of the Chapter's priceless collection of manuscripts, musical scores and early printed books.

The late 14th-century **dormitory**, 194 feet/59 metres long, is one of the most memorable claustral buildings with its grand rough-hewn timber roof. It houses the modern book collection.

The monastic library was said in the 13th century to have more books than the great Benedictine mother house at Cluny in France. Again Durham is fortunate that so much of this medieval library has survived to be enriched by succeeding generations. Precious books and manuscripts dating from the Saxon period include the Durham Gospels, a precursor to the **Lindisfarne Gospels** of which a facsimile, on display in the Treasures of St Cuthbert exhibition, was presented to the Cathedral by the British Library in 2003.

The Cloisters, Monastic Buildings and College

The book and gift shop is one of Durham's great surprises. This splendid 14th-century octagonal room with its spectacular vault was once the monastic and later the Deanery **kitchen**. The restaurant was formerly the great vaulted wine cellar (appropriately) and recalls the importance of hospitality in Benedictine life. Opposite, the **Treasures of St Cuthbert exhibition** illuminates the history of Christianity in the North-East.

LEFT Part of the Treasures of St Cuthbert exhibition

BELOW, FROM LEFT TO RIGHT 17th-century cope; seal of Henry III; St Cuthbert's portable altar

ABOVE Medieval arch leading to the College

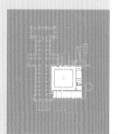

The highlights are items associated with St Cuthbert, all rare survivals from the Saxon period: fragments of his original coffin with the symbols of the four evangelists; his burial silks, vestments, portable altar, and most moving of all, the pectoral cross buried with him, surely worn by him as a bishop and a superb example of Saxon craftsmanship.

From the cloister, a vaulted passage called The Dean's Walk leads into the **College**. This is the name given in Durham to the Cathedral Close, another reminder of its monastic past and the 'college' or community of the Priory. This peaceful 'village within

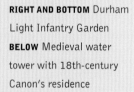

a city' is the home of the Cathedral clergy and others associated with its life, including the Chorister School where the Cathedral choirboys are educated. Many of the buildings surrounding the green originated in the Middle Ages: the Prior's Lodging* (now the Deanery), and the Priory's infirmary*, guest hall* and garner*, for example. Their remains are now incorporated into the fine 17th- and 18th-century houses that give the College its elegance and charm.

You can leave the College by the medieval gateway and walk back to the city via The Bailey; or you can return to the Cathedral via the cloister or the gift shop/restaurant entrance.

A Brief History of the Cathedral

The story of the Cathedral begins on Lindisfarne with St Cuthbert, and with the wanderings of his community of monks. They arrived at Durham with his body in 995. Within three to four years Cuthbert's body was enshrined in the 'White Church' which was finally completed in 1017. Nothing of this Saxon church remains. The first bishop of the Norman Conquest, Walcher, dissolved the Saxon community on the grounds of its alleged laxity, and replaced it with Benedictine monks who began to rebuild the monastery. His successor, William of St Carileph (or Calais), knew the magnificent Romanesque churches being built in his native France and resolved that Durham should be equally splendid. The foundation stone of the Norman Cathedral was laid on 11 August 1093. By 1104, Bishop Ranulph Flambard had completed construction down to the crossing. The rest of the nave was finished by 1133, and Bishop Hugh le Puiset's Galilee Chapel by 1189. The western towers followed early in the 13th century. The last change to the 'footprint' of the Cathedral was the building of the Chapel of the Nine Altars in the 13th century. After this, the only remaining large-scale addition was the crossing tower finished in 1487.

A watershed in the Cathedral's history was the Reformation and the dissolution of the Priory. The late medieval era is uniquely and nostalgically documented in *The Rites of Durham*, written in 1593 by a presumed one-time member of the convent. He describes the colourful ceremonies and sumptuous shrine as they had been before the monastery was surrendered to the Crown in December 1539. The Cathedral was refounded in 1541 with the last prior Hugh Whitehead as its first dean, and twelve canons who had all been monks. Much regrettable destruction of historic furnishings and artefacts took place later in the 16th century.

The Civil War and Commonwealth brought the fortunes of Durham to a low ebb. The Cathedral was closed and, after the Battle of Dunbar in 1650, Cromwell incarcerated more than 3,000 Scottish prisoners in the building. The restoration of the

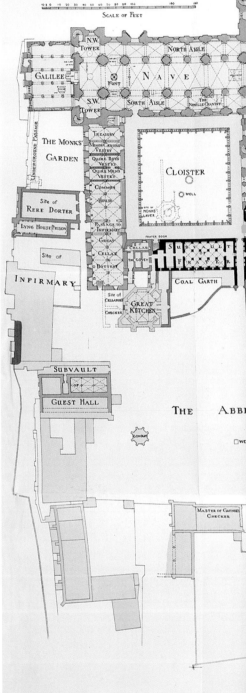

TOP LEFT AND LEFT Views of the Cathedral, **RIGHT** the nave looking east, showing the wooden organ screen taken from Architectural illustrations and description of the Cathedral Church at Durham by R. W. Billings (1843) **ABOVE** Plan of the Cathedral in colour, from The Victoria History of the County of Durham

monarchy led to the appointment of a former Canon of Durham, John Cosin, as bishop. He set about refurbishing the church with richly carved woodwork and renewing its worship. To the late 18th century we owe the rough treatment meted on the fabric: two to three inches (50–75mm) was chiselled off almost the entire exterior in order to restore the eroded surfaces, but much Norman detail was thereby lost. The Norman Chapter House was also largely demolished, and the Galilee Chapel almost lost in the interests of creating a grand entrance to the original great west door of the nave.

The next century saw the founding of the University of Durham in 1832, with endowments provided by both the Chapter and Bishop Van Mildert, who also gave the university his Durham residence, the Castle. The later 19th century left its mark in the majority of the stained glass, the rebuilt Chapter House and the Victorian furnishings in the crossing. The care that has continued to be lavished on the Cathedral in the 20th and 21st centuries has probably left it in a better state than it has ever been in its long history.

TOP RIGHT The triforium level with 19th-century cleaning techniques
FAR RIGHT West end of the Cathedral in 1672

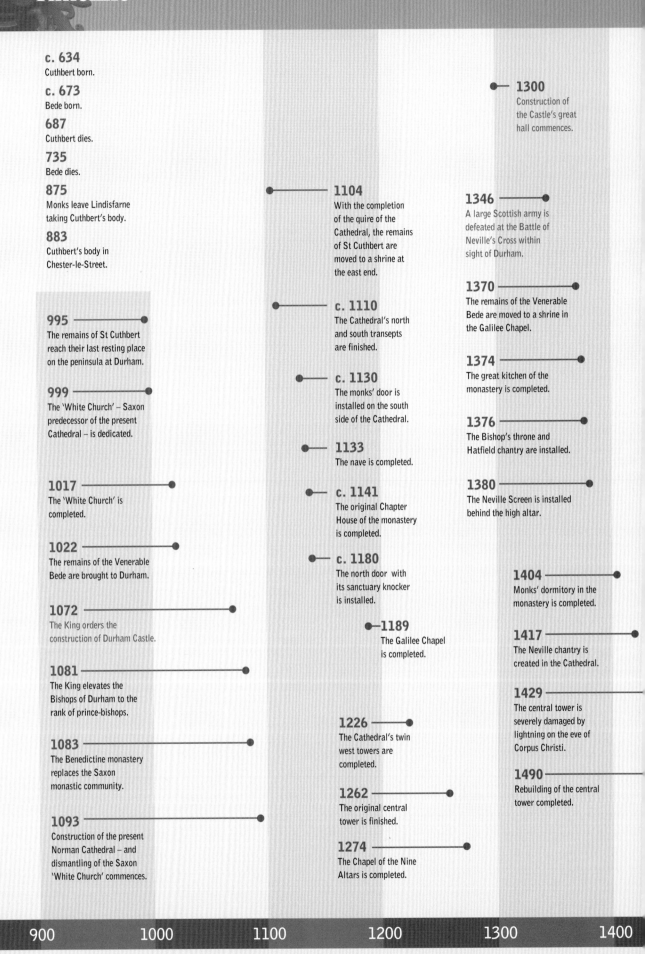

c. 634
Cuthbert born.

c. 673
Bede born.

687
Cuthbert dies.

735
Bede dies.

875
Monks leave Lindisfarne taking Cuthbert's body.

883
Cuthbert's body in Chester-le-Street.

995
The remains of St Cuthbert reach their last resting place on the peninsula at Durham.

999
The 'White Church' – Saxon predecessor of the present Cathedral – is dedicated.

1017
The 'White Church' is completed.

1022
The remains of the Venerable Bede are brought to Durham.

1072
The King orders the construction of Durham Castle.

1081
The King elevates the Bishops of Durham to the rank of prince-bishops.

1083
The Benedictine monastery replaces the Saxon monastic community.

1093
Construction of the present Norman Cathedral – and dismantling of the Saxon 'White Church' commences.

1104
With the completion of the quire of the Cathedral, the remains of St Cuthbert are moved to a shrine at the east end.

c. 1110
The Cathedral's north and south transepts are finished.

c. 1130
The monks' door is installed on the south side of the Cathedral.

1133
The nave is completed.

c. 1141
The original Chapter House of the monastery is completed.

c. 1180
The north door with its sanctuary knocker is installed.

1189
The Galilee Chapel is completed.

1226
The Cathedral's twin west towers are completed.

1262
The original central tower is finished.

1274
The Chapel of the Nine Altars is completed.

1300
Construction of the Castle's great hall commences.

1346
A large Scottish army is defeated at the Battle of Neville's Cross within sight of Durham.

1370
The remains of the Venerable Bede are moved to a shrine in the Galilee Chapel.

1374
The great kitchen of the monastery is completed.

1376
The Bishop's throne and Hatfield chantry are installed.

1380
The Neville Screen is installed behind the high altar.

1404
Monks' dormitory in the monastery is completed.

1417
The Neville chantry is created in the Cathedral.

1429
The central tower is severely damaged by lightning on the eve of Corpus Christi.

1490
Rebuilding of the central tower completed.

| 900 | 1000 | 1100 | 1200 | 1300 | 1400 |

1500
Prior Castell's clock installed
in the south transept.

1537
The King's commissioners close
down the monastery and dismantle
the shrine of St Cuthbert and the
shrine of the Venerable Bede.

1539
Durham Priory suppressed.

1541
The King refounds the Cathedral as
the Cathedral Church of Christ and
Blessed Mary the Virgin.

1545
Bishop Tunstal's Chapel and Gallery
in the Castle are completed.

1640
A Scottish army occupies
Durham and uses the
Cathedral as a barracks.

1650
Some 3,000 Scots prisoners are
imprisoned in the Cathedral by
Oliver Cromwell after the Battle
of Dunbar.

1657
Oliver Cromwell proposes to
found a University of Durham but
dies before this is accomplished.

1660
The restoration of the
Cathedral is begun.

1663
A new carved font canopy is
erected in the nave.

1665
A new screen and choir stalls
are installed in the quire.

1684
Dean Sudbury converts the
refectory into the library.

1686
The Father Smith organ is installed
on top of the quire screen.

1796
The original Chapter House
of the monastery is partially
demolished.

1827
The tomb of St Cuthbert is reopened
and several items, including his
pectoral cross, are removed.

1831
The tomb of the Venerable Bede
is reopened and a gilded iron
finger ring is removed.

1832
Bishop Van Mildert, the Dean
and Archdeacon of Durham
found the University of Durham.

1835
The Bishop of Durham loses
the status of Prince-Bishop.

1837
The University of Durham
moves into the Castle.

1840
The ruined Castle Keep is rebuilt
to house university students.

1867
The present 'Jesse' window is
installed at the west end of the nave.

1869
The present 'Te Deum' window in the
south transept is dedicated.

1876
A new quire screen and alabaster pulpit
are erected by Sir George Gilbert Scott.
The present Father Willis organ is installed.

1895
The Chapter House of the monastery is
restored as a memorial to Bishop Lightfoot.

1899
The tomb of St Cuthbert is reopened
and his remains are examined.

1923
Consecration of
the Durham Light
Infantry Chapel in
the south transept.

1947
The miners' memorial
is installed.

1952
The Castle's Norman Chapel
is restored and reopened.

1980
The Cathedral's ten bells
are rehung in a steel frame.

1984
The 'Daily Bread' window
is installed in the nave.

1993
The American Friends'
window is placed in the
Galilee Chapel.

1997
The Millennium window,
located in the south quire
aisle, is installed.

1999
Altar and icon to
St Hild dedicated.

2000
Banners of St Cuthbert
and St Oswald by
Thetis Blacker placed
in the feretory.

2003
Facsimile of Lindisfarne
Gospels given to the
Cathedral by the British
Library and
Verlag Luzerne.

2004
Dedication of Paula Rego's
painting of St Margaret of
Scotland with her son.

2005
St Cuthbert restored to
the Cathedal's dedication.

2006
St Margaret altar and
furnishings dedicated.

1500   1600   1700   1800   1900   2000

The Cathedral today

The Cathedral is a working building, as rich and complex an organism today as it was in the Middle Ages. It is a living community of prayer, hospitality, care, learning and work. At its heart lies the daily rhythm of prayer and worship.

Large-scale services take place frequently, such as the Durham Miners' Service and the annual Service for the Courts, as well as the celebration of the great festivals of the Christian year such as Christmas and Easter. As the 'seat of the Bishop', the Cathedral is a place that belongs to and is held in special affection by the Diocese of Durham. Those of other Christian traditions look to it as a church that in an important sense transcends narrow denominational boundaries. Followers of other faiths speak of how the Cathedral is truly a place for all people.

Pilgrimages provide a path towards recovering spiritual perspective. As a symbol of 'public faith' the Cathedral has key relationships with the city of Durham and its university, with the county and with the region. It provides 'sanctuary' for those in need of help or support, a place into which to bring their anxieties and concerns.

Music and the arts play a central role. The English choral tradition from the Middle Ages and the Renaissance to the present day forms the core of the choir's repertoire, though the Cathedral's music embraces almost every conceivable style as need requires. There is a rich programme of concerts, recitals and exhibitions. A lively children's education centre provides a valued service to schools in the region, with upwards of 15,000 children visiting the Cathedral every year. An adult learning programme of lectures, seminars and discussion groups benefits from the proximity of the university and its Department of Theology.

Many people are involved in caring for the fabric of the Cathedral and interpreting its heritage to visitors. The Cathedral supports a works department in which traditional skills are kept alive for the conservation of the building and the maintenance and beautifying of its grounds. The 'front of house' is served by vergers and bedesmen as well as volunteer stewards and guides. Behind the scenes, staff look after administration and the management of personnel, finance and estates. The governance and leadership of this large and complex operation belongs to the Cathedral **Chapter**, a statutory body of lay people, together with the **residentiary canons.** It is chaired by the Dean.